Barbarians!

by STEVEN KROLL *illustrated by* ROBERT BYRD

DUTTON CHILDREN'S BOOKS

For Kathleen, who kept me at it
—S.K.
For my son, Rob, and my daughter, Jennifer
—R.B.

DUTTON CHILDREN'S BOOKS
A division of Penguin Young Readers Group

Published by the Penguin Group
Penguin Group (USA) Inc., 375 Hudson Street, New York, New York 10014, U.S.A.
Penguin Group (Canada), 90 Eglinton Avenue East, Suite 700, Toronto, Ontario, Canada M4P 2Y3 (a division of Pearson Penguin Canada Inc.)
Penguin Books Ltd, 80 Strand, London WC2R 0RL, England • Penguin Ireland, 25 St Stephen's Green, Dublin 2, Ireland (a division of Penguin Books Ltd)
Penguin Group (Australia), 250 Camberwell Road, Camberwell, Victoria 3124, Australia (a division of Pearson Australia Group Pty Ltd)
Penguin Books India Pvt Ltd, 11 Community Centre, Panchsheel Park, New Delhi - 110 017, India
Penguin Group (NZ), 67 Apollo Drive, Rosedale, North Shore 0632, New Zealand (a division of Pearson New Zealand Ltd)
Penguin Books (South Africa) (Pty) Ltd, 24 Sturdee Avenue, Rosebank, Johannesburg 2196, South Africa
Penguin Books Ltd, Registered Offices: 80 Strand, London WC2R 0RL, England

CIP Data is available.

Published in the United States by Dutton Children's Books,
a division of Penguin Young Readers Group
345 Hudson Street, New York, New York 10014
www.penguin.com/youngreaders

Designed by Beth Herzog

Manufactured in China   First Edition
ISBN 978-0-525-47958-1   10 9 8 7 6 5 4 3 2 1

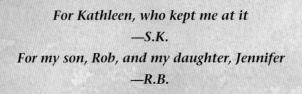

Are you rude, crude, and uncivilized? Could you be—a barbarian?

The ancient Greeks used the word barbarian to describe anyone who did not speak their language or share their culture. The Romans used the word for people who lived beyond their borders, people they considered coarse or simply foreign. The Roman Empire stretched over most of Europe, lasting from 27 B.C. to 476 A.D. But as the Romans grew weaker and the empire divided into east and west, unruly groups like the Goths and the Huns began invading them. The Romans used the word barbarian a lot during those later years.

Eventually barbarian came to mean anyone who was rude or coarse, but over the centuries many groups have been labeled barbarians. The four that influenced civilization the most were the Goths, the Huns, the Vikings, and the Mongols.

But were these people as barbaric as we've been led to believe they were? We know they killed a lot of people and took over whole countries. We know they looked a little like the armies in a fantasy movie. But we also know the Romans could be cruel, and because the barbarians could not read or write, we don't have their side of the story.

Often historical events are written about long after they have taken place. History is recorded by people miles, even countries, away from the settings of those events. How can we know who's telling the truth, especially when there always seems to be someone stretching it?

What we do know is that these four barbarian groups marched across Europe and Asia and brought both together through trade and conquest. They opened the world to new ideas and cultures and made it larger and more dazzling. Without them, our lives might have been very different.

Contents

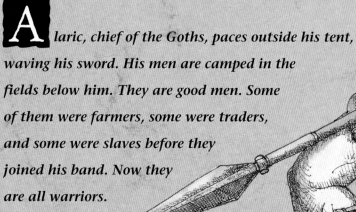

laric, chief of the Goths, paces outside his tent, waving his sword. His men are camped in the fields below him. They are good men. Some of them were farmers, some were traders, and some were slaves before they joined his band. Now they are all warriors.

They left their homes to follow Alaric to Greece and then to Italy. Along the way, they stole treasure when they found it and killed anyone who tried to stop them. Now they are camped on a hill outside Rome.

The men have been waiting for action for many months and are growing restless. Instead of fighting an enemy, they are fighting with each other. Alaric has demanded that the enemy give the Goths gold and corn. He wants to be made a general in the Roman army. Those are to be the payments for peace. But no word has come from the leaders of the Roman Empire.

Now is the time, Alaric says to himself. Tomorrow the Goths will destroy Rome. The date is August 24, 410 A.D.

THE

4

Goths

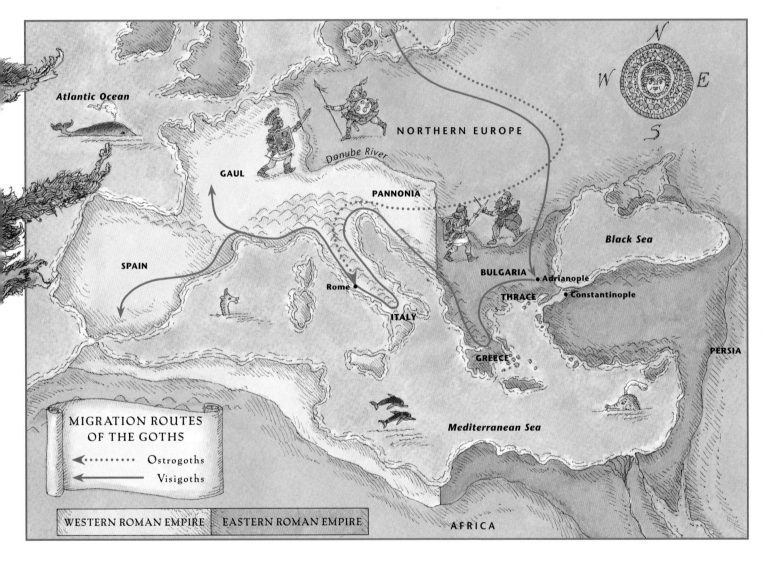

MIGRATION ROUTES OF THE GOTHS

←········ Ostrogoths

←——— Visigoths

WESTERN ROMAN EMPIRE | EASTERN ROMAN EMPIRE

The Goths were Germanic tribes that left northern Europe in the second and third centuries to settle in the south, near the Black Sea. While we are not certain why they migrated, it was probably for better farmland and a warmer climate. In the fourth century, the Goths lived on the borders of the huge and powerful Roman Empire. Initially, the Goths and Romans lived in relative peace as neighbors. But when the Goths were attacked by the Huns, they wanted the Romans to protect them. The result was war and the beginning of the end of the Roman Empire.

Ice skates made from bones were common in the ancient northern lands. Leather thongs tied the bones to the bottoms of shoes.

This Ostrogothic cloak pin combines a bird design with a cross. The intricate metal design is set with garnets.

A Way of Life

In peaceful times, the Goths built their villages in a ring or rectangle around a central pasture. They lived in timber and wattle houses and in wooden huts built over holes in the ground. The holes were used either to store goods or to deposit trash.

When farming, the Goths used a new method called crop rotation, which meant growing different crops on the same fields from year to year. This helped renew the soil. Using manure as fertilizer produced bigger and better harvests.

The Goths ate mostly grain and only a little meat. They preserved their meat with salt to keep it from rotting. Drinks were brewed from barley and cherries and then spiced.

Feasting was a favorite way to celebrate victories and festivals. The Goths held contests with swords and bows to test the skills of their warriors. In winter, they went skating on bone skates. They liked music and dancing and could not get enough of gambling, boasting, and quarreling.

Goth men wore short cloaks or tunics and sometimes trousers. The women wore capes and dresses, and bronze and gold jewelry in bird or animal designs.

Warriors carried shields, but body armor and horses were rare. They fought on foot, naked to the waist.

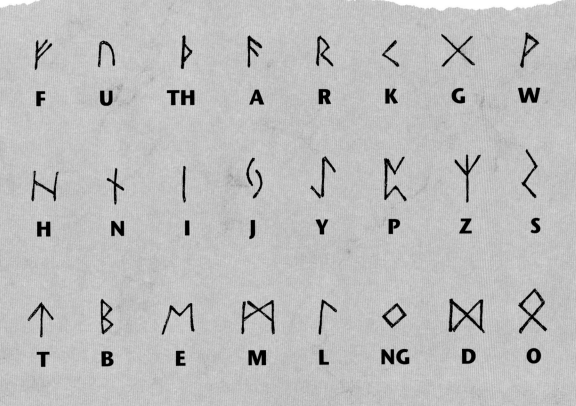

F	U	TH	A	R	K	G	W
H	N	I	J	Y	P	Z	S
T	B	E	M	L	NG	D	O

This alphabet, for one of the earliest Germanic languages, is called the futhark and is made up of symbols called runes. The runes stand for different sounds and were considered to have magical power by the Gothic people. The language based on the futhark was simple and could not be used to convey complicated ideas.

In the fourth century, Bishop Ulfilas developed the written Gothic language by adding letters from the Greek and Latin alphabets to the Germanic futhark. He was then able to translate the advanced ideas of the Bible into the new Gothic language and bring Christianity to the Goths.

𐌿𐌽𐍃𐌰𐍂
unsar
our

𐌰𐍄𐍄𐌰
atta
Father

𐌸𐌿
thu
thou

𐍅𐌴𐌹𐌷𐌽𐌰𐌹
weihnai
hallowed be

𐌽𐌰𐌼𐍉
namo
name

𐌸𐌴𐌹𐌽
thein
thine

𐌹𐌽
in
in

𐌷𐌹𐌼𐌹𐌽𐌰𐌼
himinam
heaven

Above is a section of The Lord's Prayer, taken from the Ulfilas translation, with the correct pronunciation and the English version below it.

A Force for Living

The Goths were tall people with long heads and red or blond hair. They followed a religion based on nature known as paganism. Goths believed in the worship of many gods. Nerthus was the goddess of the earth. She made the crops grow.

The chief god was Odin, pictured as an old man with a beard and only one eye. He was the god of war, and had two raven messengers named Hugin (thought) and Munin (memory). They flew around the world to bring Odin all the news of the day.

Odin was also the father of poetry and the inventor of the runes, or alphabet symbols. Supposedly, the magic of the runes could heal the sick or protect a person from harm.

Yule was the pagan festival of the winter solstice (when the sun is farthest south from the equator). Yule lasted twelve nights, from December 20 (Solstice Eve) to December 31 (New Year's Eve). When Christians wanted to combine the Yule festival with the birth of Jesus, they chose to make December 24 Christmas Eve.

The idea of Santa Claus originated with the god Odin riding his eight-legged steed Sleipnir through the sky on the "wild hunt" of the winter months. During Yule, pagan and other Germanic children left straw and sugar in their shoes to help Sleipnir guide Odin. In return, Odin left them gifts.

Ostara was the pagan goddess of spring and beauty. Christians did not feel they could demonize her the way they did other pagan gods because she represented purity and innocence. Christians adapted Ostara's holiday celebrated on the Spring equinox—when day and night are of equal length—into Easter. Both holidays included the fertility symbol of rabbits and the ritual of coloring eggs.

Goths and the Roman Empire

In 376 A.D., the marauding nomadic tribes of the Huns attacked the Goths from the east. Two groups of Goths—the Tervingi and the Greuthungi—fled to the Danube River, along the northern border of the Roman Empire.

By this time, the Roman Empire was divided into two portions, the East and the West, with two different emperors. The Goths were looking for protection inside the Eastern Empire.

Valens was the Roman emperor in the East. He wasn't sure he should let the Goths in. He decided to let in only the Tervingi, and only if they would accept the Christian God and the government in Rome.

The Fight Begins

The Tervengi had *no* choice. Valens said they would be given food, farmland, and peace, but they were kept in camps and starved. Many, including children, were sold into slavery in exchange for food.

Then a Roman army leader invited the Goth leaders to dinner and tried to kill them. One escaped. The other disappeared. The Gothic people grew angry. They still had their weapons, so thousands of Goths attacked and defeated the Roman army leader and his men.

The Goths began stealing and fighting to get food. Valens had to fight back. He prepared to battle the Goths at the city of Adrianople on August 9, 378.

Valens's scouts had given him faulty information. He did not know that the Goth army was so large or that they were well armed. When his soldiers met the enemy, they panicked. Valens and two-thirds of his army were killed.

Alaric and Rome

Moving from town to town, the Goths continued stealing until a new emperor, Theodosius, took the place of Valens. Theodosius wanted to offer a truce to the Goths. If Goths would serve in the Roman army, he said he would give them land in northern Bulgaria. The Goths accepted Theodosius's offer.

To the Romans, the Goths were still crude and dangerous. They remembered their loss at Adrianople. On the battlefield, Goth soldiers serving in the Roman army were pushed to the front and were the first to die.

The Goths felt betrayed again. Then in 395, thirteen years after the agreement, Theodosius died. The Goths came together under their new leader, Alaric. Angrily he led them through Greece and Italy, destroying everything in his army's path. Finally Alaric reached the city of Rome, the heart of the Roman Empire.

Alaric made his demands but never heard from the Roman leaders. He and his men seized the city and its riches, but to him, his victory meant nothing. If he didn't get the respect and acknowledgment of the Roman leadership, what did it matter that he had seized Rome? He stayed three days and left.

By the end of the year, Alaric had died from disease in southern Italy. He was only forty years old.

Alaric did not take over the Roman Empire, but he did join together the Tervingi with other Gothic tribes. They became the Visigoths, which meant "the good, the noble." The Visigoths settled throughout Gaul and Spain where they practiced Roman law and order.

Ostrogoths

But the Visigoths were not the only Goths. Remember, some Goths were never allowed into the Roman Empire. When the Greuthungi tribes finally freed themselves from the Huns, they became the Ostrogoths, which meant "Goths of the Rising Sun." In 484, the Ostrogoths joined together behind a new leader, Theodoric the Amal.

Theodoric was a dealmaker and a strong general. He fought against the eastern Roman emperor, then took over Italy and became King Theodoric the Great.

As a boy, Theodoric had spent years within the Roman Empire. He liked Roman ways and made his kingdom strong in Roman law, education, and Christianity. He gained more and more power. In 511, he took over the entire kingdom of the Visigoths and reunited the Gothic people.

When Theodoric died in 526, his empire began to fall apart. His daughter briefly became queen because her son was too young to be king, but she was murdered in her bath. By 561, the eastern Roman Empire had once again taken over Italy.

Gone but Not Forgotten

Gothic civilization finally ended with the Arab invasion of the early eighth century. But over twelve hundred years later, their influences are still around. The term Goth is now used to explain a specific type of architecture (which critics thought inferior), a type of scary story, and even a youth subculture that is known for dressing in black clothing.

Yet history remembers the Goths as the people who hastened the end of the Roman Empire. Strangely, they would also preserve the law and culture of that empire and spread them to faraway places.

A ring with the likeness and name of Alaric the Goth

A gold coin with an image of Theodoric

A bronze gilt German medallion with an image believed to represent the god Odin

The sun rises over the Morava River, near the city of Margus in the Balkan Peninsula. Roman soldiers gallop up to a group of Huns and jump to the ground. Bleda and his younger brother, Attila, watch from their horses.

Bleda and Attila are the leaders of the Huns. The eastern Roman Empire agreed to pay the Huns in gold to keep peace in the area, but the Romans have stopped paying. The Huns have come to demand payment.

"We will talk to you from here," Attila says.

Although the Huns are known for never getting off their horses, the Romans find this rude and are furious. Still, they mount their horses again to negotiate with the Huns. Attila and Bleda demand that the Romans raise the amount of payment to 700 pounds of gold a year.

The year is 435 A.D. Attila has only begun to seize power.

14

THE Huns

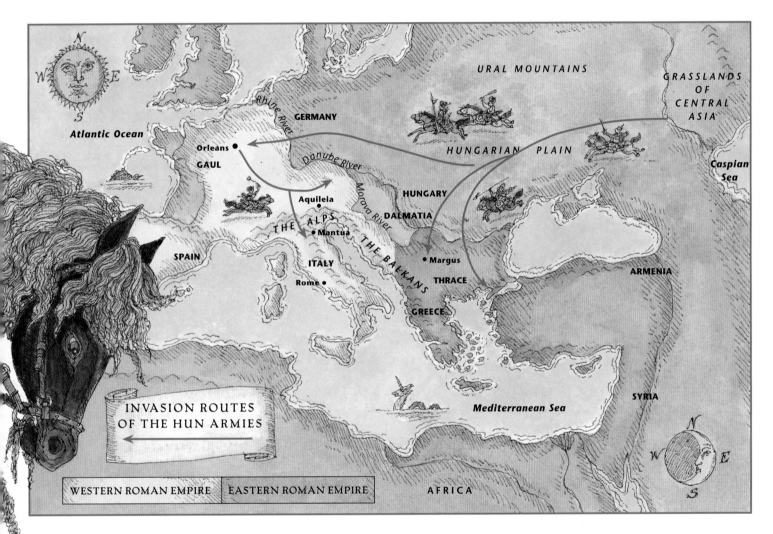

 In the last quarter of the fourth century, the Huns came pouring into Europe from out of the east. They robbed people and destroyed towns, spreading panic and fear through Eastern Europe.

The Huns slashed their faces with swords to make themselves look more frightening. They wore round caps and odd clothes made of ragged linen and marmot skins.

Always moving from place to place, the Huns were nomads—they had no permanent home. They came from the grasslands of Central Asia and seemed to live on their horses. These horses—small, shaggy creatures—could survive on grass alone. Fighting battles on horseback was the Huns' greatest talent. How they used that talent to gain power and wealth changed the history of Europe.

Wanderers

Hun families traveled in large wagons with wooden wheels rimmed with iron. Because they were not farmers, they had to count on grazing their herds and hunting for food.

Hun rulers had many wives. The first wife and her children were given special privileges in Hun society. Families lived in round tents made from horsehair. A group of tents made up a camp. A group of camps made up a clan, and a few clans made up a tribe. Their religion was based on daily experiences. They made sacrifices to fire, water, and the moon. They also worshipped gods of the road for safe travel and animals they found unusual or remarkable.

But the Huns' lives revolved around horses and weapons. Their saddles had comfortable wooden frames for easier riding. Warriors traveled with extra horses so there would always be a fresh one when the other tired. They carried long, double-edged swords and lassos. The Huns developed the reflex bow, which bent farther and had more pull, allowing arrows to fly up to five hundred feet and still kill an enemy soldier.

The Huns used stirrups, so they did not need their hands to hold their horses. They would race out in front of an army as if being chased, then stand in their stirrups and fire behind them.

Warriors and Deal Makers

In 376 A.D., the Huns attacked the Goths north of the Danube River. That was when the Tervingi Goths crossed the river into the Roman Empire. Using clever planning and their savage skills with swords and bows, the Huns conquered the Greuthungi Goths.

In the winter of 395, Hun warriors attacked the Roman Empire for the first time. In their unending pursuit of power and loot, the Hun army crossed the frozen Danube River and terrorized the Roman provinces of Thrace and Dalmatia. Then moving south and east, they overran parts of what is now the Middle East.

Soon Huns were also swarming across the middle of Europe, but even as they fought the Romans, they made deals with them. The Romans knew that in some cases it was easier to "buy peace" with gold, an especially useful tactic since the Huns would spend the gold on Roman goods. Sometimes the Huns would force the Romans to make deals with them by taking wealthy hostages. These important Roman citizens would be held as prisoners until the Huns got their way. One of these hostages was Aëtius, who would later become a Roman general.

Hunnish youths practiced fighting skills from an early age.

Bleda and Attila

At the beginning of the fifth century, most of the Hun tribes were living on the Hungarian plain. They controlled an empire that stretched from the Ural Mountains of Russia almost to the Rhône River in western Europe.

Rugila, their leader, had joined together many of the Hun tribes. Rugila's warriors wiped out a band of Romans on the lower Danube and invaded Thrace yet again. There the eastern Roman emperor, Theodosius II, offered Rugila three hundred and fifty pounds of gold a year if he would make peace. Rugila accepted.

Eleven years later, the Huns provided soldiers to help a Roman general, Aëtius, the same Aëtius who had once been their hostage. To show his gratitude, Aëtius gave Rugila a part of the Roman Empire in what is now Hungary.

The Huns, long wanderers and conquerors with no home of their own, finally had a homeland that no one could dispute. They even began farming. But in 434, Rugila died. Now the tribes were ruled by his two nephews, Bleda and Attila.

Attila Seizes Power

Bleda and Attila didn't like it when the eastern Roman Empire stopped paying them for peace. But after their successful talks on horseback, the Romans and Huns signed the Treaty of Margus, which provided the Huns with payments of gold, trading rights, and the return of Hun prisoners. With a treaty in place, Bleda and Attila were able to concentrate on conquering areas in the Alps and along the Rhine River in what is now Germany. But five years later the peace was broken when the Huns claimed that the Bishop of Margus helped Romans rob Hun graves. The Huns offered to spare the bishop's life if he left the gates of Margus open as he escaped. They swept in through the open gates and conquered the city.

Attila and Bleda went on to take most of the Balkan Peninsula. But the two brothers, with very different personalities, had constant disagreements. So much so that in 445, Attila murdered Bleda and became the sole ruler of the Huns.

The Huns believed in seers and shamans (priests who practiced magic) and in a ritual called *scapulimancy.* Scapulimancy foretold the future by burning the shoulder blades of dead animals and then examining the cracks in the bones.

High-ranking Hun families displayed their wealth by wearing jewelry such as this gold looped fibula. Decorated with gemstones, the fibula acted like a giant safety pin to fasten garments of men and women. Its insect shape was believed to have magical powers and was used to ward off evil.

Attila the King

Attila had been a Roman hostage and knew Roman ways. He thought that if the Huns were to become a great power, they must learn from successful societies. That was why many of his advisers were foreigners. Attila could be friendly to visiting diplomats, but that did not stop him from his goal of conquest. The Roman historian Priscus said that Attila "was born to shake the races of the world."

Honoria

In 447, for power and loot, Attila captured the rest of the Balkans. Earthquakes and terrible storms stood in his way, but he kept going. By that time, almost all of Europe was in his grasp. Treasure and gold offerings had made the Huns and Attila rich.

But then, his plans went wrong.

Honoria, sister of the Roman emperor in the West, was told to marry a rich senator named Herculanus. She didn't want the marriage. She sent a servant to Attila with her ring and a letter, begging him to rescue her.

The real meaning of Honoria's letter seemed to be: Marry me, and I'll make you emperor of half the western Empire! The Roman emperors in the east and west were not going to give up any power, but Attila believed they would. He wrote them both, saying he was going to marry Honoria and should be given half of the western Roman Empire.

The emperors refused him.

Gaul

Meanwhile, the Huns had decided to conquer Gaul and the Visigoths. The western Roman emperor, angry at Attila for accepting Honoria's ring, ordered his army to help the Visigoths. That army was led by Aëtius, Attila's former friend.

All the armies of Western Europe were now fighting Attila together.

On June 14, 451, the Huns were forced back from the city of Orleans. Barely a week later they were beaten again at Châlons. According to legend, Attila fell back into a circle of wagons and built a huge pile made of saddles. If the enemy broke through the circle, he would set fire to the saddles and jump into the blaze. Attila wouldn't be taken alive.

But Aëtius told the Visigoths to go home and let the Huns escape. He did not wish to destroy Attila and his army because they might somehow still be useful to him and the Romans.

The Scourge of God

Now there was a new Roman emperor in the East. His name was Marcian, and he refused to continue paying the Huns for peace.

Attila was angry about that, but he was angrier at the western Romans for helping to defeat him in Gaul. He attacked and destroyed the cities of Italy as far south as Mantua. There he faced a group led by Pope Leo I in the summer of 452. Aëtius arranged the meeting.

Pope Leo had called Attila the "Scourge of God." He said God would be good to the Huns if they didn't attack Rome, the holy city. Attila listened, but he had already decided not to attack Rome. Everywhere in Italy, people were starving. The plague, a fatal disease spread by rats, was rampant. He couldn't risk losing an army to an enemy he could not fight. He had decided to take his men home.

The End of the Huns

While still in Italy, Attila decided to marry again. On his wedding night, he burst an artery in his sleep and died.

Attila was buried in a secret place along the Tisza River on the Hungarian plain. To this day the site remains a mystery. There was no one to take his place. Attila's many sons were not good at ruling. The Hun Empire fell apart.

The Huns changed the face of Europe by forcing groups like the Goths to flee and migrate to other lands. In their short history, they did not leave many other accomplishments. Still Attila is remembered because his actions contributed to the end of the Roman Empire and because the Hungarians consider him a hero. Also he has been featured over the centuries in plays, operas, and even movies. There have been many warrior kings, but Attila will always be the Scourge of God.

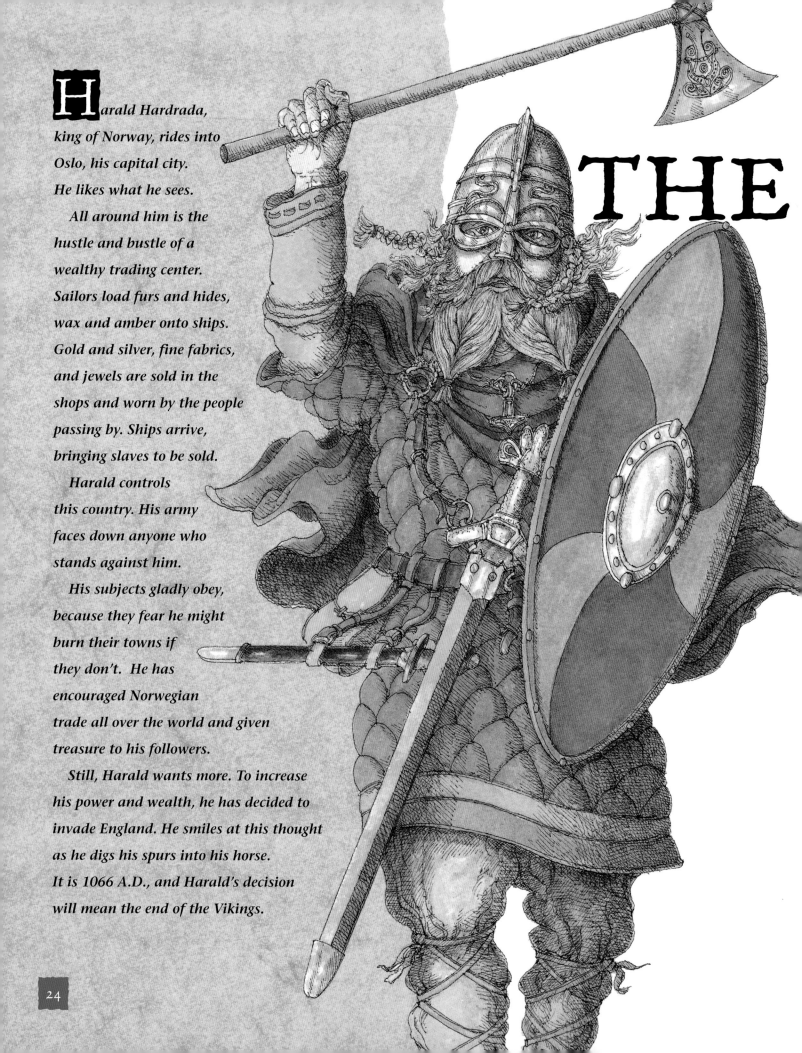

Harald Hardrada, king of Norway, rides into Oslo, his capital city. He likes what he sees.

All around him is the hustle and bustle of a wealthy trading center. Sailors load furs and hides, wax and amber onto ships. Gold and silver, fine fabrics, and jewels are sold in the shops and worn by the people passing by. Ships arrive, bringing slaves to be sold.

Harald controls this country. His army faces down anyone who stands against him.

His subjects gladly obey, because they fear he might burn their towns if they don't. He has encouraged Norwegian trade all over the world and given treasure to his followers.

Still, Harald wants more. To increase his power and wealth, he has decided to invade England. He smiles at this thought as he digs his spurs into his horse. It is 1066 A.D., and Harald's decision will mean the end of the Vikings.

THE

Vikings

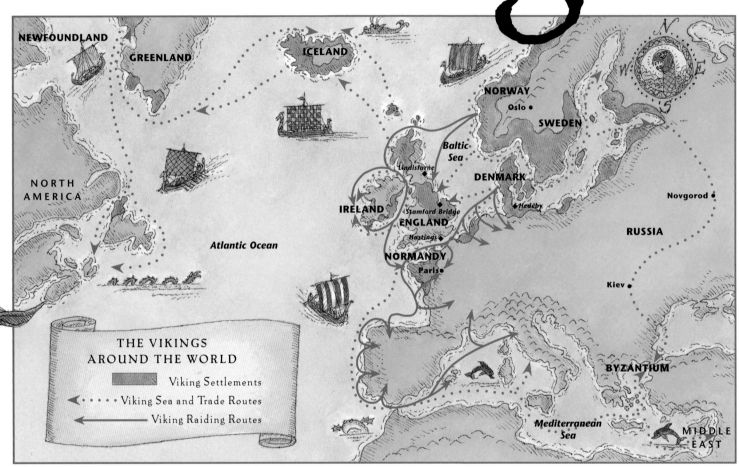

THE VIKINGS
AROUND THE WORLD

▬ Viking Settlements

◄····· Viking Sea and Trade Routes

◄───── Viking Raiding Routes

From 793 to 1066 the Vikings ruled the northern seas. They were known as bloodthirsty pirates and raiders, stealing and killing to increase their own wealth. But the Vikings were also explorers, traders, and shipbuilders who traveled from Russia to the Middle East and even reached the coast of North America.

The Vikings came from the three present-day countries of Scandinavia: Norway, Sweden, and Denmark. These countries, which lay northeast of England, have a harsh climate.

Most of the land is mountainous, which made farming difficult. The season for growing crops is short, and winters are brutal. Livestock were kept in sheds to keep them from freezing.

The same rugged conditions that made farming hard also made travel a problem. All three countries are almost completely surrounded by water. Because of this, Scandinavians found it easier to travel by ship rather than by rough mountainous land. This hard life and love of the sea set the stage for the age of the Vikings.

A Way of Life

The invention of the Viking longship made the age of Viking conquest and exploration possible. Longships had many different designs. Some had six oars on each side. Others had as many as twenty. The ships were smooth and solid. Their sails were easy to handle, and they didn't sit deep in the water. They were strong for carrying goods and fast for fighting battles.

In battle, there was nothing better. The ship could travel up the narrowest river and slip onto a beach, bringing men to the heart of the action. Then the crew could turn the sail into the wind and start rowing to ensure a quick escape. They could outrun nearly every enemy sailing ship.

Promises of great riches tempted Scandinavian men to "go Viking." Poor and constantly at war with one another at home, they set sail in their longships to raid and steal and conquer other people's land.

Vikings needed to sell their spoils from raids, so they also became traders. Market towns were built where trading ships could reach them, but also where they could be protected from pirates. Hedeby was such a town on a narrow arm of the ocean called a fjord in southern Denmark. It had a massive wooden pier in the harbor and a wall made of earth around three of its sides. The sea protected the fourth side. The wall and the pier kept the streets and homes safe.

Vikings lived in wooden homes with a large central room. The houses usually had either a very small window or none at all. There was a large fire continuously burning in the center of the house with a hole in the ceiling to let smoke escape. Small rooms connected to the main house might be used for cooking or storage or to keep livestock. During the day the house was used for weaving or cooking; at night Viking families slept on long benches that lined the walls.

Viking Beliefs and Law

Each of the three Viking nations spoke versions of the Old Norse language. These were so similar that people from all three nations easily understood one another. Like the Goths, the Vikings used runes as their written language. They also shared the gods of the Old Norse religion—there was the chief god Odin; Thor the warrior, who caused thunder and lightning; and Frey and Freya, the god and goddess of fertility. The Vikings had many spiritual myths and legends to explain the world. All of them centered on a giant ash tree that held the universe.

Viking society had three classes of people: the free (including craftsmen and farmers), those who were slaves (captured during Viking raids), and those who were in charge (kings and nobles). All had to follow the rules approved at "the Thing"—the governing group of freemen that met to create and discuss laws. It was the earliest known lawmaking body in Europe.

The chess piece above portrays a berserker. This marauding Viking warrior is depicted chewing his shield. Beserkers would wear animal skins into battle and work themselves into such a frenzy that they appeared to be insane. Some people believed berserkers were invincible warriors on the battlefield.

Stones were decorated with runes that were cut or engraved with decorative figures. Some of them were painted in bright colors. They told stories and showed scenes from mythology.

Yggdrasil, according to Viking mythology, was the great ash tree holding the nine levels of the Norse universe together.

1. Gimle: The high heaven with a roof of stars and jewels. An eagle sits on the top branches of Yggdrasil, keeping watch.

2. Asgard: Home of the gods

3. Vanaheim: Home of the vanir, who send soft winds and showers

4. Alfheim: World of the elves, spirits of light and fertility

5. Jotunheim: Glacial home of the Jotuns, the rock and frost giants, and of the many-headed trolls

6. Midgard: The Earth, home to humans surrounded by an ocean where Jormungard, a giant serpent, lived. Bifrost was a flaming rainbow bridge to the world above. Three Norns controlled the destiny of humans. They healed the wounds of the tree with sacred water.

7. Svartalfleim: The world of dwarves and dark elves. Skilled miners and smiths, they supplied the gods with silver and iron.

8. Niflheim: Frozen world of fog and ice; The Land of the Dead, where the hag, Hel, ruled over all those not killed in battle. Nidhogg, the dragon of destruction, gnaws at Yggdrasil's roots. Ratatosk, a nosy squirrel, delivers insults between the eagle and the dragon.

9. Muspelheim: Land of fire and home of the fire demon, Surt

ALFHEIM

MUSPELHEIM

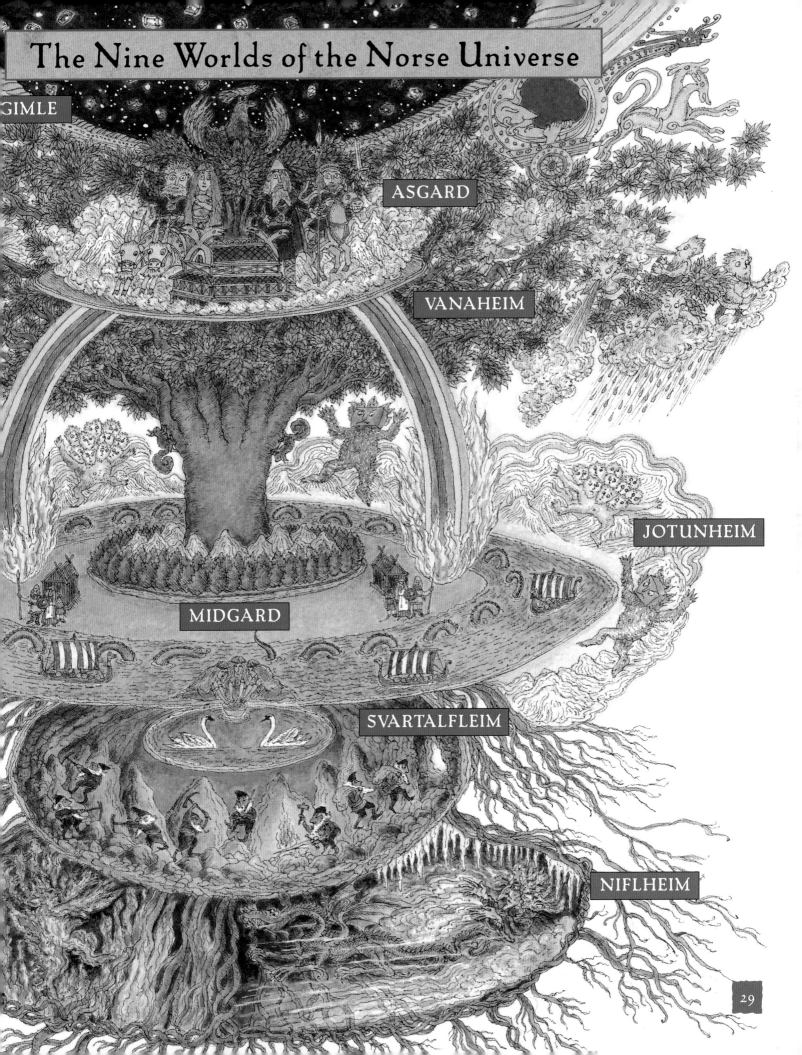

The Nine Worlds of the Norse Universe

GIMLE

ASGARD

VANAHEIM

JOTUNHEIM

MIDGARD

SVARTALFLEIM

NIFLHEIM

First Attack

The first Viking attack came from Denmark. The Danish Vikings made the raid outside their own country on St. Cuthbert's monastery in Lindisfarne, on the east coast of England. Churches and monasteries held treasures of silver and gold that were not protected by armies. The monks were no match for these villains. The date was June 19, 793 A.D. The Viking Age had begun.

Normandy, Russia, England, Iceland

In 845 A.D., Danish Vikings attacked Paris. King Charles the Bald of France bribed them to stop the looting and killing. Instead of stopping the Vikings, the bribe only encouraged more raids and more bribes throughout Europe.

Vikings soon took over parts of Normandy in France. At the same time, Swedish Vikings, called the Rus, were traveling by rivers and other waterways to help build powerful cities in Novgorod and Kiev in what is now Russia and Ukraine.

The Vikings also headed west. Danes settled along the east coast of England. Norwegians went to Ireland, and by 870, they began settling Iceland. Iceland was a barren island and had nothing to trade. But it had wonderful natural resources like wild blueberries, plentiful fish, and seafowl. The Norwegians decided to create a settlement there. To this day the language spoken in Iceland is similar to the medieval Norwegian language that the Viking settlers spoke.

Greenland

Erik the Red was a criminal. He was thrown out of Norway, and then banished from Iceland for three years, beginning in 982. He spent those years exploring a new country to the west. He called it Greenland.

But Greenland wasn't green. It was gray and cold. This didn't matter to Erik. When his banishment ended, he returned to Iceland and gathered four hundred and fifty people, most of them social outcasts like himself, and took them to settle in Greenland. They set up a national assembly similar to the one they knew. They farmed, hunted, and traded, and the community eventually grew to five thousand people. Four hundred years later the settlement ended when temperatures in the northern hemisphere plummeted during a period of exceptionally cold weather called the Little Ice Age, and survival became nearly impossible.

An Icelander named Bjarni Herjolfsson was the first to see North America in 986. He sailed past by accident, trying to find Greenland. But around the year 1000, Leif Erickson, son of Erik the Red, followed Bjarni's path. He traveled south instead of north and received credit for discovering Newfoundland—almost five hundred years before Christopher Columbus would land in North America.

This carved stone shows Viking warriors attacking the monastery of Lindisfarne, or the Holy Isle, off the English coast in 793.

The Vikings did not wear those helmets with cattle horns sticking out on the sides that we see in advertising and the movies. Enemy combatants could have grabbed hold of them. They wore cone-shaped helmets made of leather. Only their leaders wore metal helmets and coats of chain mail.

The earliest crucifix from Scandinavia—made in the tenth century of wired gold and hammered metal—reflected the coming of Christianity to the Viking lands.

Harald Hardrada (1015-1066)

Harald Hardrada was the perfect example of a Viking. He was a well-traveled military man, joining battle when he was just fifteen years old under his half-brother King Olaf Haraldsson of Norway.

In the year 1030 Olaf was killed in battle (he was later sainted for bringing Christianity to Norway). In that same battle, Harald was wounded but escaped to live with family in Russia. There he served under a distant relative named Jaroslav the Wise. Harald wanted to marry Jaroslav's daughter but was gently refused and told he was not wealthy enough. Harald offered his fighting services to the Byzantine Empire.

There he became a great general, fighting throughout Europe and in the Middle East. He also gathered a fortune from his many raids.

During his time in Byzantium, Harald heard that Olaf's son, Magnus the Good, had been made king of Norway. Harald believed that he, as the half-brother of Olaf, had the right to share power equally with Magnus. Escaping the Byzantine army, he went back to Russia to ask again for Jaroslav's daughter's hand in marriage. This time his request was granted. Then he made his way back to Norway with his new wife.

After Harald had led several raids through territories ruled by Norway, Magnus agreed to share his kingdom with him. But Magnus died less than a year later, and Harald became the sole king of Norway.

The End of the Vikings

Nothing stood in the way of the new king. He killed his enemies and gave favors to those who supported him. But then Harald insisted upon taking over England.

The Battle of Stamford Bridge took place north of York in England on September 25, 1066. Harald Hardrada was surprised by Harold God-winson, now the English king. No one knows if the Norwegian forces just weren't ready, but the battle was long and bloody. Harald Hardrada was killed by an arrow to the throat.

While the English finally won, they were too tired and had lost too many soldiers to fight again. A few days later, they lost the Battle of Hastings and their kingdom not to Vikings but to the Normans and their leader William of Normandy.

It was the beginning of a new age of trade and exploration. The Vikings had played a major role in making these changes happen. Their long-ships created trade routes all over Europe and east into the lands that would become Russia. Their trade brought foreign customs and traditions all over the world. But the Vikings were also settlers, carving out communities in Iceland and Green-land, reaching North America, and helping to develop settlements in England and Normandy. Without them, the medieval world would have remained smaller for much longer.

The horse comes charging into camp. The rider falls from his back. It is Yisugei, Mongol clan leader, father of Temuchin.

"I'm dying," Yisugei says between gasps. "Tartars—they poisoned me . . ."

The Tartars are the sworn enemies of the weaker Mongols, but there is a custom that says strangers on these grasslands must always be treated as friends. The Tartars have broken this custom with poison.

Yisugei has been off with another Mongol tribe, looking for a bride for Temuchin, his oldest son. Now he is dying.

One of his aides brings Temuchin home from another camp. The boy is powerless to help as his father lies on his deathbed. But Temuchin, the future Genghis Khan, will never forget this moment or his thirst for revenge.

THE

Mongols

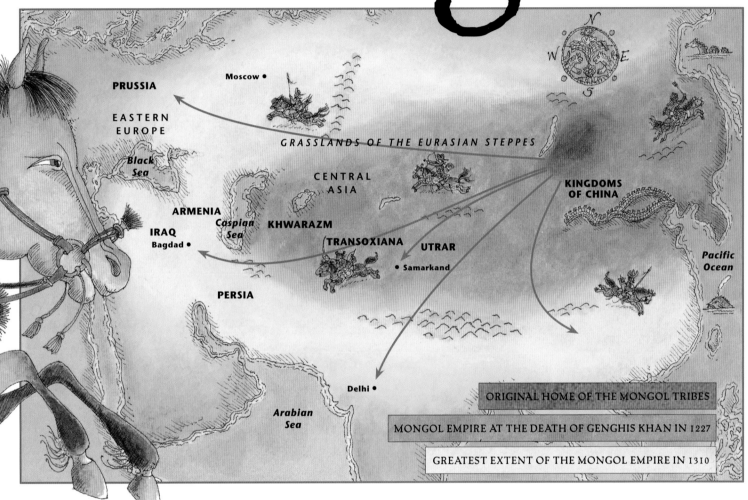

PRUSSIA

Moscow •

EASTERN
EUROPE

*Black
Sea*

GRASSLANDS OF THE EURASIAN STEPPES

N
W *E*
S

CENTRAL
ASIA

KINGDOMS
OF CHINA

ARMENIA

*Caspian
Sea*

KHWARAZM

IRAQ
Bagdad •

TRANSOXIANA

UTRAR

*Pacific
Ocean*

• Samarkand

PERSIA

Delhi •

ORIGINAL HOME OF THE MONGOL TRIBES

*Arabian
Sea*

MONGOL EMPIRE AT THE DEATH OF GENGHIS KHAN IN 1227

GREATEST EXTENT OF THE MONGOL EMPIRE IN 1310

In the middle of the twelfth century, on the vast grasslands of the Eurasian steppes between Persia, Central Asia, and the kingdoms of China, lived the wandering tribes of Mongolia. Poor and constantly at war, these tribes wore the skins of horses, sheep, and camels. At the eastern end of the steppe lived the Mongols and the Tartars.

No one knows exactly when Temuchin, the future Genghis Khan, was born, but most scholars believe 1167 A.D. From the humblest origins he began uniting steppe tribes to help create the largest adjoining land empire in world history. But as a youth, he would be tested. After his father's death, Temuchin's life unraveled. It would be many years until, older and stronger, Genghis Khan would begin to change the world.

Temuchin and the Mongol Way of Life

The Mongols were nomads. They traveled from sheltered valleys in winter to pastures on the plain in summer. They lived in easily carried tents called *yurts*. The cloth for the yurts came from sheep's wool. It was pounded into felt cloth which was waterproof and very sturdy. Mongols relied on their sheep not only for yurts, but also for food and clothing.

With Yisugei dead, his clan needed another leader. They did not choose Temuchin, his son, and even worse, they abandoned their former leader's family. To survive, Temuchin, his mother, and his siblings were forced to gather berries and hunt as they moved from place to place on their own.

As Temuchin grew older, he did not forget what had been done to him and his family. He found friendship with the Kereit tribe and offered his services to their leader, who had been a childhood friend of Temuchin's father. The leader welcomed him and eventually helped Temuchin to regain his rightful place within his clan. Temuchin came to believe not only in his revenge against the Tartars but in his future as a leader.

Unity, Revenge, Power!

As he grew older, and more magnetic, Temuchin gathered other Mongol leaders around him and became a gifted chieftain. He inspired loyalty and treated his own people generously, showering them with gifts and showing them kindness. The Mongols began to see him as their champion. He did not come from royalty. Though his father had been a clan leader, Temuchin was born a shepherd. He was one of them and they felt that the spirits were on his side.

After several years, Temuchin succeeded in uniting many of the Mongol tribes, and he became their khan, or leader. In 1196 he was ready for his revenge against the Tartars.

Like the Huns, the Mongols were excellent horsemen and used the powerful reflex bow. Mongols were also smart soldiers. They could draw an enemy into a trap by pretending a retreat, or put dummies on spare horses to make it seem that their army was larger than it was.

The Mongols and Temuchin eventually crushed the Tartars and subdued other tribes of the steppe. By 1206, Mongol nobles declared Temuchin the Genghis Khan, or "universal leader."

Touring troupes of dancers, acrobats, and entertainers performed remarkable feats in the court of Genghis Khan.

Falconry was a favorite sport among the wealthy. Genghis Khan considered the gift of a falcon one of the highest compliments that could be paid him.

The Mongols had knowledge of astronomy and planetary movements. The shamans were believed to have predicted eclipses of the sun and the moon. They threw sheep bones into fires and predicted events based on the cracks in the bones. The arrangement of thrown sticks by soothsayers was supposed to foretell events.

Genghis Khan was said to know magic and to go into a trance before any important decisions were made. Anything he said during the trance was recorded, and he would act according to these words. He once stayed in his yurt for four days, communing with the spirits about an upcoming battle in China.

Organizing the Mongols

The Mongols were an independent people, and it would have been hard for any leader to stay in control. But Genghis Khan was not just any leader. He organized the Mongol army into groups of ten, one hundred, one thousand, and ten thousand followers so that orders could flow easily from him to every soldier. At the head of each group was a *Chiuliarch* whose authority was greater than that of the old tribal leaders. Eventually Genghis Khan organized the entire nation in similar fashion. There was no longer tribal loyalty—there was only loyalty to Genghis Khan.

Law and Religion

Genghis Khan created a set of his own laws to guide the Mongols, called the Great Yasa. It provided instructions for family conduct, property, the army, relations with other nations, and the collection of taxes. Peace and order were the most important goals of the Great Yasa. Anyone guilty of lying would be put to death.

Genghis Khan was generous when it came to religious freedom, allowing others to worship in their own faiths without fear of his army. He himself believed in traditional Mongol shamanism.

Shamanists worshipped gods in Heaven, but believed that spirits in the world controlled man's fate. The shaman—or priest—went back and forth between the world of the gods and the world of men, using magic to cure illness and predict the future. Genghis Khan was as fearful of the future as any of his followers. He believed in the magical world of the shaman and always asked advice at a shrine before leading his army into battle.

China and Central Asia

With the Mongols united, Genghis Khan's followers became restless. They wanted more victories and more treasure. Tempted by the riches, Genghis Khan invaded the kingdoms of China. First he subdued the weaker kingdom of Hsi-Hsia in the northwest. In 1211, he began an invasion against the more powerful Chin Empire. But the Chin proved to be a tough enemy. It would be twenty-three years before the Mongols finally conquered all Chin lands. Genghis Khan would not live long enough to see that victory.

Meanwhile in Central Asia, Sultan Ala al-Din Muhammad of Khwarazm had three Mongol merchants killed, accusing them of spying. Genghis Khan sent three trusted followers to the sultan, demanding that something be done

to make up for the outrage. Not knowing the strength of Genghis Khan's army, the sultan answered by killing one of the followers and shaving off the beards of the other two.

To the Mongols, this was an unacceptable insult. Genghis Khan declared war. Refusing to entrust his troops to just one leader, Sultan Ala al-Din Muhammad split them among different cities. The Mongols defeated each unit, one by one. Finally Samarkand, the sultan's capital, fell. The sultan fled, only to die in exile.

Death and After

As a warrior, Genghis Khan destroyed everything in his path, spreading salt on fields to destroy crops and knocking down cities that would not give up. Much of what he destroyed was never rebuilt.

In the summer of 1226, old and ill, Genghis Khan set out for China. In August 1227, while battling in Hsi-Hsia, he died. His empire at the time of his death extended from the Caspian Sea all the way to what is now Beijing. Two years later, Genghis Khan's third son, Ogedei, was elected Great Khan. Two other sons and a grandson shared portions of the empire: the original Mongol homeland, the lands in Central Asia, and everything to the west.

Ogedei went on to invade Eastern Europe and to take over the lands in southern Russia that became known as the Golden Horde. It was he who finally defeated the Chin Empire. Years later Kublai Khan, a grandson of Genghis Khan, conquered the Song dynasty, brought all three kingdoms together, and created the Mongol-controlled Yuan dynasty of China.

Tamerlane

After Ogedei's death, there were struggles for power among the Mongols. Three brothers, grandsons of Genghis Khan, became the clear winners. Mongke ruled first and sent another brother, Hulagu, to conquer parts of Muslim Asia. Hulagu led the bloody siege of Baghdad in 1258. Kublai would become the last Great Khan.

One hundred years later, Kublai was dead and the Yuan dynasty over. A new leader, Tamerlane, arose. A Mongol and Muslim by birth, he took over Transoxania and declared he was bringing back Genghis Khan's empire.

Tamerlane went on to lead his army into Moscow and to conquer all of eastern Persia, Armenia, Georgia, and Iraq.

A master of Genghis Khan's military style, Tamerlane was known for his brutality, even stacking up the skulls of his victims. But he spared the artisans and engineers in the lands he conquered and brought them to Samarkand to create amazing gardens and an enormous mosque. In 1398, Tamerlane destroyed Delhi in India and went on to even more victories. But that wasn't enough. Claiming to be the rightful heir of the Yuan emperors, Tamerlane wanted to conquer China, but like Genghis Khan, he never did. He died on his way there in 1405.

Legacy of the Mongols

The Mongols became part of the fabric of many of the regions they conquered. But more important they linked Europe, the Middle East, and Asia and opened up trade routes. The Mongols began an age of discovery that would help link nations and create the modern world.

Time Line

100–300 A.D.   *Tribes of Goths move from Poland to the Balkans, north of the Black Sea.*

376 A.D.   *Attacked by the Huns, Goths flee to the Roman Empire.*

378 A.D.   *Goths defeat Roman Emperor Valens at Adrianople. He and two-thirds of his army are killed.*

410 A.D.   *Alaric and his Goth followers sack Rome. Later, Alaric dies in southern Italy, but he has united Gothic tribes that become the Visigoths.*

493 A.D.   *The Ostrogoth Theodoric murders his rival Odovacar at a banquet and becomes King of Italy.*

100 A.D.

526 A.D.

561 A.D.   *The eastern Roman Empire takes over Italy.*

The Goths

The Huns

526 A.D.   *Goth leader Theodoric dies. His empire begins to fall apart.*

375 A.D.   453 A.D.

484 A.D.   *Freed from the Huns, Gothic tribes have become the Ostrogoths.*

453 A.D.   *On his wedding night, Attila bursts an artery in his sleep and dies.*

445 A.D.   *Attila murders his brother Bleda and becomes sole ruler of the Huns.*

375 A.D.   *The Huns come pouring out of the east, spreading panic and fear in Eastern Europe.*

1066 A.D. Harald Hardrada invades England and is defeated by the English king at the Battle of Stamford Bridge, north of York. A few days later, the English lose the Battle of Hastings and their kingdom to William of Normandy. The Viking Age has ended.

1370 A.D. Tamerlane murders his partner, becomes sole ruler of Transoxania, and begins his reign of terror, attempting to restore the empire of Genghis Khan.

"93 A.D. Danish Vikings plunder St. Cuthbert's Monastery n Lindisfarne on the east coast of England. The Viking Age f conquest and exploration has begun.

1167 A.D. Temuchin, the future Genghis Khan, is born.

845 A.D. Danish Vikings attack Paris. King Charles the Bald bribes them to desist, which encourages more Viking attacks all over Europe.

1206 A.D. Temuchin becomes Genghis Khan—the "universal leader"—and sets his sights on conquering China.

3 A.D.

1066 A.D.

The Vikings

The Mongols

1167 A.D.

1405 A.D.

1405 A.D. Tamerlane plans to invade China but dies before he can get there.

1000 A.D. Leif Erickson, son of Erik the Red, gets credit for discovering Newfoundland and creating a link for the Vikings between North America and Europe.

1227 A.D. After conquering most of Asia and the Middle East, Genghis Khan dies on his way to final victory over the northwest Chinese kingdom of Hsi-Hsia.

986 A.D. Erik the Red establishes a settlement in Greenland.

1196 A.D. Temuchin finishes uniting many of the Mongol tribes and begins his revenge on the Tartars.

Bibliography

The Goths

Heather, Peter. *The Goths.* The Peoples of Europe Series. Oxford: Blackwell Publishers, 1996.

Pennick, Nigel. *The Inner Mysteries of the Goths, Rune-Lore & Secret Wisdom of the Northern Tradition.* Berks: Capall Bann Publishing, 1995.

Todd, Malcolm. *Everyday Life of the Barbarians.* London and New York: B.T. Batsford Ltd. and G.P. Putnam's Sons, 1972.

Wolfram, Herwig. *History of the Goths.* Berkeley, CA: University of California Press, 1988.

The Huns

Blacklock/Kennet. *The Roman Army.* New York: Walker & Co, 2004.

Harvey, Bonnie Carman. *Attila the Hun.* Philadelphia: Chelsea House Publishers, 2003.

Howarth, Patrick. *Attila, King of the Huns: The Man and the Myth.* New York: Barnes & Noble Books, 1994.

Ingram, Scott. *Attila the Hun, History's Villains.* Farmington Hills, MI: Blackbirch Press, 2003.

Laing, Jennifer. *Warriors of the Dark Ages.* Gloucestershire, UK: Sutton Publishing Ltd., 2000.

Lawrence, D. H. *Movements in European History.* Cambridge: Cambridge University Press, revised ed., 2002.

Nicolle, David and Angus McBride. Color plates. *Attila and the Nomad Hordes.* Oxford: Osprey Publishing Ltd., 1990.

Owen, Olwyn. *The Sea Road.* Edinburgh: Congate Books Ltd., 1999.

Simons, Gerald. *Barbarian Europe. Great Ages of Man.* New York: Time-Life Books, 1968.

Thompson, E. A. *The Huns.* The Peoples of Europe Series. Oxford: Blackwell Publishers, 1996.

The Vikings

Christiansen, Eric. *The Norsemen in the Viking Age.* The Peoples of Europe Series. Oxford: Blackwell Publishers, 2002.

Clements, Jonathan. *A Brief History of the Vikings: The Last Pagans or the First Modern Europeans?.* New York: Carroll & Graf, 2005.

D'Aulaire, Ingri and Edgar. *Norse Gods and Giants.* Garden City, NY: Doubleday & Co., 1967.

Jones, Gwyn. *A History of the Vikings.* Oxford and New York: Oxford University Press, 1968; reissued 2001.

Margeson, Susan M. *Viking.* Eyewitness Books. New York: Dorling Kindersley, 1994; revised, 2003.

Tryckare, Tre. *The Viking.* Milan: Officine Grafiche di Enrico Berinzagli & Co., 1966.

Wingate, Philippa, and Dr. Anne Millard. *Viking World.* London: Usborne Publishing Ltd., 1993.

The Mongols

Bell-Fialkof, Andrew, ed. *The Role of Migration in the History of the Eurasian Steppe.* [City]: Palgrave Macmillan, 2000.

De Hartog, Leo. *Genghis Khan: Conqueror of the World.* New York: Barnes & Noble Books, 1989.

Editors of Time-Life Books. *Timeline 1200-1300, The Mongol Conquests.* Alexandria, VA: Time-Life Books, 1989.

Morgan, David. *The Mongols.* The Peoples of Europe Series. Oxford: Blackwell Publishers, 1986.

Ratchnevsky, Paul. *Genghis Khan: His Life and Legacy.* Translated and edited by Haining, Thomas Nivison. Oxford: Blackwell Publishers, 1991.

Roux, Jean-Paul. *Genghis Khan and the Mongol Empire.* New York: Harry N. Abrams, 2002.

Illustrator's Note

The most challenging aspect of working on Barbarians! was finding the information needed to create the illustrations. What did these people look like? Where did they live? How did they live? When dealing with antiquity, there is only so much visual material available to the researcher, and in most circumstances the imagery and impressions discovered are from an earlier time and there is not necessarily any guarantee of accuracy. I tried to be as thorough as possible in my depiction of these people and their environments. I found more information on the Vikings and Mongols than on the Goths, and very little about the Huns. I tried to create the world of these societies as faithfully as I could imagine them in their historical settings, with the references available to me. In a way, I was confronting ghosts, and ghosts don't usually reveal too much.

Robert Byrd, 2008

Acknowledgments

With special thanks to my intrepid editor, Steve Meltzer, who left no stone unturned, and to everyone who contributed so much to this book: our designer - and resourceful researcher - Beth Herzog; our art director, Sara Reynolds; our associate editor, Margaret Woollatt; our copyeditor, Rosanne Lauer; and, for her expertise on Mongol history, Kim Dramer.

Steven Kroll

To the staff of the Haddonfield Public Library for the invaluable help they have given me for many years.

Robert Byrd

Index